COCO CHANEL

COCO CHANEL

THE STYLE PRINCIPLES

HANNAH ROGERS

Unofficial and unauthorized

SIMON
ELEMENT

Intro

duction

Chanel.

There are few brands better known or more desired in the world. It is a name even the least fashion-literate individual will recognize; its double-C logo, to many, is a symbol of the industry itself, imbued with status and glamour. But how much do you know about the woman behind it—and where did her founding style principles come from?

This book seeks to answer that question. It is by no means an exhaustive history or biography of Coco Chanel. Rather, it takes a closer look at the designer's most famous creations—all of which were revolutionary for women's wardrobes at their conception—to seek out ten style lessons that can be applied to a contemporary wardrobe. Woven together, those diktats piece together her fundamental fashion theory: that women's clothing should be as wearable as it is beautiful. It should enhance, not hinder; liberate, not restrict. Each chapter will look at how we can be inspired by that philosophy and make it work, practically, when we get dressed.

The psychology of this goes back to the designer's very beginnings. Gabrielle Bonheur (later "Coco") Chanel, the brains behind some of the most expensive perfume, clothing, and accessories in the world, had a start in life that was not buoyed by the perks of wealth and privilege, but poverty and pain. She was born on August 19, 1883, in a hospice for the needy in France, the daughter of humble market traders. And from eleven years old, she as good as had to fend for herself: her mother died, her philandering father abandoned her, and she was sent to an orphanage run by nuns.

A fairy tale it was not. But it shaped her outlook on life and the clothing she thought women should wear when taking it on: elegant but practical; simple but effective. This is not something the designer would have ever cared to admit. Chanel was incredibly evasive about her early life; journalists and biographers have found her tricky to pin down, for her stories often changed. She sought to keep the truth about her childhood in the shadows and the details of her affairs and relationships blurry. Perhaps, that considered, it was inevitable that she would become a fashion designer: an individual with the power to weave dreams within seams.

She used her style to set herself apart, then imposed it on the world. During an era of corsets and cumbersome crinolines for women, she preferred and popularized trousers and tailor-made boxy jackets. Many of the items she iconized were inspired by the wardrobes of her male lovers, which she preferred for their straightforwardness and comfort. She did not feel that overtly expensive things suited her and that was translated into her minimal designs: Chanel made monochrome, masculine tailoring, sensible shoes and handbags you

could wear on the body, rather than clutched, must-haves. At the time, these items and ideas were entirely novel.

She was the first of her kind: a so-called New Woman of her era. Chanel never married (by choice, but also circumstance—she turned down proposals but never got one from her great love). She had legendary love affairs with myriad famous men, but died alone in her suite at the Ritz in Paris at eighty-seven years old, on January 10, 1971. She did so financially liberated and independent by her own means, just as she had lived her adult life. She was a legend of her time, famous all around the world—an original influencer.

She was also democratic in her design. Chanel more often than not took humble, unfussy items and translated them with a lift for her wealthy clientele. That's rather the spirit of this book: you don't need a bottomless bank account to get the Chanel look. Chances are you already have it in your wardrobe—you just need to know where to look (and how to wear it).

embrace

MILLINERY

"A woman's education consists of two lessons: never leave the house without stockings, never go out without a hat."

Coco Chanel

A n It-bag. Must-have shoes. Glossy, thick-rimmed, logo-stamped sunglasses. A wallet. These are the accessories that are most likely to spring to mind when we think about Chanel. They are what we see plastered on billboards and on double-page spreads in magazines. They are what get artfully modeled by carefully selected famous faces on red carpets and "unboxed" (that's unwrapped, for the Insta-illiterate) by influencers for likes and shares on social media platforms.

They are the items that we, the consumer, are most likely to covet—or, certainly, aspire to afford—from a luxury designer. That's why accessories are the bread and butter of big-brand profit buffets. They offer a gateway into the world of luxury fashion and are sold at what its sentinels consider

Étienne Balsan

Étienne Balsan was a wealthy textile heir who met Chanel just as she was embarking on her adult life. From working as a seamstress, living above a shop—and reveling in the nightlife of Moulins—she was invited to come and live with him at his family estate: a former abbey named Royallieu. Chanel stayed there as a kept woman and mistress until she met Boy Capel.

entry-level price points (though as anyone who has wistfully browsed a Chanel website will know, those are still pretty steep to mere mortals).

What you might not know, though, is that the original must-have accessory from Chanel was in fact not a quilted lambskin handbag or two-tone, cap-toed heel. It was a hat. That's right. Coco Chanel's first foray into fashion was as a milliner. What started as a hobby of making and selling hats to friends in her twenties—something she did to fill her time while living as a kept woman in the chateau of the French textile heir Étienne Balsan—turned into a business in 1910 when Chanel, just shy of thirty years old, opened Chanel Modes in Paris at 21 rue Cambon. She did so with the financial backing of Balsan and her first great love, Arthur "Boy" Capel.

Hats were very much part of the uniform for fashionable women at the time. To step out without one would have been considered a social faux pas. This was at the tail-end of *la belle époque*, a period in France characterized by economic prosperity, hedonism, and optimism. For fashion, that meant extravagance: society coquettes, as they were known, were trussed up within an inch of their lives. Everything women wore in that period was ornate, frilly—and quite cumbersome. Hats were typically lavish and rather heavy.

But not Chanel's. It was her view that a woman could not properly use her brain if her head was being weighed down. That's why her hats stood out for being, as with all of her fashion designs to follow, determinedly unfussy. The beauty of her designs was in their simplicity. In fact, the very first Chanel hats were humble straw boaters—purchased from the Parisian department store Galeries Lafayette and then trimmed by the designer with ribbon.

The fact they lacked an ostentatiousness did not stop them catching the attention of famous actresses of the day. Rather, it had the opposite effect—they were considered something new and exciting (not to mention downright practical). Soon, everyone wanted a hat made by Coco Chanel. Her business flourished to the point where she no longer needed money from the men who had originally backed her. In 1913, just three years after the launch of Chanel Modes, the business was prosperous enough for Mademoiselle Chanel to start designing ready-to-wear, and later the iconic accessories we most recognize today.

But park all that for now. The hats are important. They are where Chanel's fashion journey began and how her core style principle of pared-back elegance was first commodified. In the century since, and under the guard of subsequent creative directors, hats have never left Chanel collections. The item may no longer be something every woman grabs before they walk out of the door, but there is rarely a Chanel catwalk without some sort of headwear, be it a beret, snood, or headband. Millinery is a cornerstone of the brand identity—and just as important is how to style it.

Arthur "Boy" Capel

Arthur "Boy" Capel was the Englishman who stole the young Coco Chanel's heart. A wealthy polo enthusiast and playboy, Boy met Coco in 1906, riding horseback, while Chanel was living at Royallieu, Balsan's home. They were lovers for nearly a decade (even when Capel was married to someone else). He died unexpectedly in a car accident, breaking Chanel's heart.

Turning Heads

Not all hats are created equal—certainly not through the lens of Coco Chanel. Were we to adopt her approach to choosing a hat, the standout styles would be those that come with all the look and detail of a luxury item without sacrificing comfort. They would at once elevate and simultaneously be everyday. Most importantly, they would never, ever be boring.

There is a great deal of joy to be found from looking at how Chanel's favored hat shapes have been reimagined on the brand's catwalks over the years. Karl Lagerfeld, the now legendary German designer who took the helm at Chanel in 1983 and stayed there for nearly four decades, was a master of the art. His hats had a sense of humour—and in turn, occasionally veered from his predecessor's rules about wearability. On his Autumn/Winter 1984 catwalk, for example, models wore red double-C stamped ice-hockey helmets; and supermodel Naomi Cambell's head was adorned with a giant pile of fluff-tastic fuchsia feathers for the show of Spring/Summer 1994.

Such styles might work on the front row at Fashion Week, but certainly wouldn't in real-world terms (not for your average supermarket shopper anyway). And, to that point, I think it is natural to feel a bit unnatural in a hat. It is an item we tend to reserve for big life events or posh days out—see Ascot, Henley, and the Princess of Wales at church on Christmas Day. With the exception of a woolly pom-pom iteration during cold snaps, putting a hat on can feel a bit, for want of a better word, *extra.*

So much of this is tied up in whether or not you are someone who thrives on turning heads. Inevitably, wearing a hat means you naturally take up more space in the world—it adds both height and breadth to one's presence. Chanel was someone who was in favor of this, but her greatest skill was making it look effortless. It was her view that a hat could give one gravitas and power—so much so that she once suggested everyone should wear one to lunch with someone they don't know, for it gave the wearer an "advantage."

Shape

There is a science to finding your perfect hat. The British milliner Awon Golding advises trying on a great number and doing so in a full-length mirror: hats are part of a full outfit and in many cases are the dominating item in an ensemble. She also advises a rule of thumb of not wearing a hat wider than one's shoulders if you want to proportion your silhouette.

Following that, your hat search should start with working out which might be the most flattering shape, something that will vary depending on your face. Those with a **long or oblong face**, for example, will best suit wide-brimmed styles and anything that cuts across the forehead, such as a beret, so as to shorten the proportions of the face. **Square faces** will look great in those too, as well as a cloche, a style often seen on Chanel catwalks.

Berets, boaters, and newsboy caps work on those with a **heart-shaped face**. If you have a **round face**, you need something that will create length and angles: medium- to long-brim fedora or trilby styles work nicely. You could also style a beret farther back on your hairline which will create length. **Oval faces**—lucky things—can get away with anything.

long or oblong

square

heart-shaped

round

Color

The design of the hat matters too. I personally believe that hats look best in block colors or metallics. Chanel would agree. While her creations might have had contrasting details or adornments, they would never have been garish. Further to that, a block color will be easier to style with the rest of your outfit, and with many other outfits. It will have a timeless, ever-after quality that will have you pulling it out of the wardrobe again and again.

How you choose that color will vary depending on your skin tone. It goes without saying that anything worn as close to your face as a hat should be chosen in a color that complements you, just as you would jewelry, lipstick, or shade of hair dye. Skin tones fall into four groups (cool, warm, olive, and neutral) and can be determined by doing the paper test on the next page.

Your Skin Undertone

In a naturally lit area, place a piece of white paper next to your face. If your skin looks pinkish next to it, you have **cool** undertones. If it looks yellow, you are **warm**. If it's green you see, you have **olive** undertones, and if you see no undertone at all, you are **neutral.**

PINKISH

you have

cool

undertones

&

You suit black, gray, silver, blues, purples, reds with blue bases, and blue-greens.

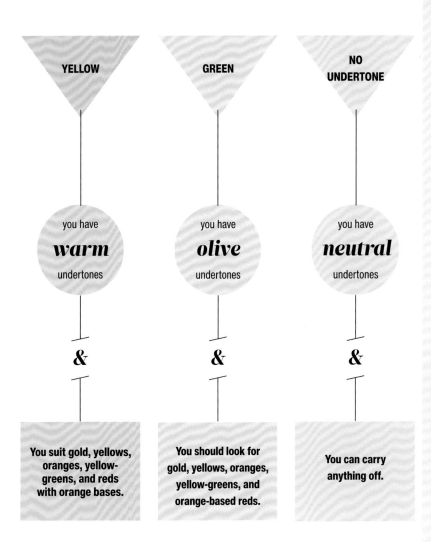

YELLOW

GREEN

NO
UNDERTONE

you have

warm

undertones

you have

olive

undertones

you have

neutral

undertones

&

&

&

You suit gold, yellows, oranges, yellow-greens, and reds with orange bases.

You should look for gold, yellows, oranges, yellow-greens, and orange-based reds.

You can carry anything off.

Texture

Finally, consider what your hat is made of. When I think of a Chanel accessory, I think of sumptuous fabrics, velvet, stiff felt, grosgrain ribbon. At whatever price tag you choose, you want it to look expensive. Avoid wool that will bobble easily or plasticky, fake leather.

Keep It Simple

As for what to wear with your hat, my suggestion is to keep it simple. You'll read that advice a lot in this book, but that's the point: simplicity was in the very essence of Chanel's style. To that end, the best way to decide if a hat is for you is to get in front of a mirror in it. You have to play around a bit to find what works. For example, I know baseball caps look terrible on me—but not when worn backwards.

It is all about experimenting. Most importantly, it is about how you feel; what Golding calls the "experience" of wearing that hat. By Chanel's rules, the point of millinery is to give its wearer confidence. In it, you should want to walk with your head held high. Anything less would undermine her ethos—so don't force anything that feels silly (and maybe avoid the hot-pink feathers).

Go black & white but
NEVER BORING

"Black has it all. White too. Their beauty is absolute. It is the perfect harmony."

Coco Chanel

T he House of Chanel and its creations have never lacked color. On the contrary—a quick glance at the brand's website from season to season will proffer pops of cherry red, azure blue, jade green, yellow, and fuchsia (and that's just the handbags).

Personally, Chanel always brings a particular shade of sugar-spun pink to my mind. This has nothing to do with my preference for the color and everything to do with the number of supermodels I have seen wearing it to great effect, from Claudia Schiffer's 1995 campaign for the brand (Schiffer poses coquettishly, blow-dry fanned out, in baby-pink plat-form sandals, sequin bralette, tweed miniskirt, and high-waisted underwear, sunglasses held aloft in one hand and cropped suit jacket in the other) to Naomi Campbell on its Spring/Summer 1993 runway in a pink tweed minidress and jacket, pink streaks punk-ishly flowing in her hair, to German model Anna Ewers on the cover of February 2021's *Vogue* Paris, wrapped in a bubblegum-pink Chanel cardigan dress, pink mini quilted handbags layered on each hip. Perhaps we might call it the Barbie effect.

I digress. This chapter is nothing about pink. In fact, I think Mademoiselle would scoff at the thought. For there were two colors she upheld over all others, as much on principle as simply a matter of taste. You need only to look at Chanel packaging to know which they are, or the House's flagship stores on the smartest shopping streets in the world. What else, but black and white?

The little black dress. Two-tone pumps. The black quilted leather handbag. White gowns designed not for virginal brides, but post-Depression party girls. Chanel's most iconic designs came in monochrome. She loved black and white, even when the tones were not considered fashionable. There are a number of hypotheses as to why, many of which are tinged with sadness and linked to an early life defined by poverty and abandonment that Chanel went to great lengths to conceal.

One, for example, attributes it to a sort of post-traumatic scarring from seeing her mother's dead body being covered in a white sheet when Chanel was eleven years old. Another is that black and white are the color of habits—just like those worn by the nuns who ran the orphanage Chanel and her sister were dropped at by their uninterested father after that very event. Those nuns cared for Chanel until she was eighteen years old and it is thought that they taught her to sew.

Then, there is the grief that engulfed Chanel following the death of Boy Capel. On December 22, 1919, Capel—who was by this point married to Lady Diana Wyndham but still

Coco Chanel in white sillk and pearls, 1931

very much in the thralls of his near decade-long affair with Chanel—was killed in a road accident. Chanel had felt grief before this tragedy. Certainly, it was something she carried around with her for most of her life. But Capel was a monumental love and to lose him caused the designer a near insurmountable grief. One can't help but attribute this to the fact she spent the decade that followed creating evening gowns in the color of mourning: black.

But was it grief, or was it a reaction to the world around her? Only Chanel knew the answer to that. But here's what we do know: Chanel had a knack for sensing cultural shifts. All great designers do. There is an art to predicting what consumers want before they want it; to making the unexpected desirable.

Which brings us to October 1926. Vibrant color was in fashion at the time, as a reaction to all the gloom of postwar life. It was three years prior to the Great Depression—a time of severe economic challenges worldwide that would lead the upper classes to wear their wealth with a little more *stealth*. American *Vogue* hit the newsstands with the debut of an item of clothing that would change how women get dressed forever. It was Chanel's LBD. Yes, *that* LBD—the Little Black Dress.

The page shows a sketch of a model wearing a black, long-sleeve, calf-length, crêpe de chine shift. It is worn loose—no hourglass figures here; Chanel's look, as per her own body shape, was boyish—and finished with a string of pearls, black cloche hat, and matching black court shoes. By all accounts, it cuts a modest shape. Beneath, *Vogue* writes "here is a Ford signed 'Chanel,'" comparing it to the car manufacturing giant's practical, accessible, and widely identifiable Model T.

It goes on to say that the dress would become, "a uniform for all women of taste." That might make sense now, but keep in mind that prior to this, black dresses had mostly been reserved for mourning and servants. They were designed for women to hide behind; to shroud and render the wearer invisible. In the hands of Chanel, it was transformed into a cult item; something every woman of status wanted to wear to make a statement. Her LBDs were seen as sexy: they had asymmetric hemlines, low decolletage flashing necklines or backs, details designed to catch the eye. She had, in her own words, successfully, "imposed black."

A vogue for white evening wear came soon after, a sartorial reaction to the economic gloom of the Great Depression. Chanel had embraced it long before that—she loved to wear white. The designer may have never married, but a satin gown in the shade was far more to her than simply an item to be given away in: it was something she could use to stand out from the crowd. It was, to her mind, ethereal and glamorous—not a sign of purity. She was a great lover of white pajamas at parties and all-white looks in situations where it wasn't quite practical. On the society scene of the 1930s, Chanel's gowns were hugely popular and, in the face of the Wall Street crash, her business boomed. The color held such rapture over her that her 1933 Spring collection came in white alone. Three decades later, well into the Swinging Sixties, it was still making up a large chunk of her collections, particularly on short cocktail dresses, which she would offset with sequins and pearls and silk taffeta sashes in different colors.

A Sense of Order

As a stylist, I love color—working with it on shoots and wearing it day-to-day. My favorite fashion week is Copenhagen because the Scandinavians have such a playful way with every shade (sometimes wearing them all at once). And while black and white might not be the most exciting colors on the chart, I concede that they do offer one thing over all else when it comes to getting dressed: order. Yes, the stain stakes are high in the latter, but you cannot get much wrong wearing black and white.

They look great alone and worn together. They are, by and large, flattering. They can be worn on days we don't feel much like being seen at all (we all have them) and, at the other end of the spectrum, when we want to stand out. Above all, they are easy. Why else were fashion editors once so known for their penchant for black on the show circuit that they earned the nickname "the crows"?

Contemporary Monochrome

Wearing the colors in a contemporary way, though, is a different matter. The highly reputable personal stylist Anna Berkeley, who has worked in the fashion industry for nearly three decades and dresses women from every walk of life, says her clients still seek out black as an easy, chic, and slimming option. She says LBDs allow the wearer to stay simply dressed but advises styling them with contrasting accessories. I think this is key: an LBD can easily look ageing in my book or, dare I say it, dull. I would also advise seeking out designs that have interesting details if you are set on one: an asymmetric hem or neckline, cutouts, interesting architecture.

Head-to-Toe Black

Head-to-toe black looks should get the same treatment, per Berkeley. She cites statement collars, embellishment, or interesting stitching as ways to modernize a monochrome outfit. I also think it is wise to mix up your textures: try black leather or patent trousers with a cotton T-shirt or sweater; a black silk shirt with black jeans. The Front Row set makes use of this trick all the time at Fashion Week—you get all the benefits of wearing one color (it is flattering, namely) without your outfit actually lacking interest.

All White

White is a different beast. Personally, I think it can look very modern and very cool: all-white outfits have long been popular with the wealthy one percent of society (those who spend their time around pristine white yachts, tablecloths, and carpets) but you see them more and more on stylish types on the train these days. I think this is because white has lost its somewhat preppy—perhaps tacky, too—connotations of old. But only if you play by the new rules.

White jeans, for example, are tricky—Berkeley even says she is downright dubious about them. We agree that skinny and jegging iterations are to be totally avoided, while wide-leg styles look marvellous. White T-shirts are a must-have, but they look best boxy. Crisp white shirts are eternally stylish; most of all, I think, when in a boyfriend shape and starchy cotton poplin weave. White shoes are acceptable now, but never stilettos: think ankle boots, loafers, and low-heeled slingbacks and sandals. Lots of fashion editors I know get white manicures, but even these come with rules: they look best on short nails, not acrylic talons. All of these things, it goes without saying, come with the usual warnings about stains and scuffing, which will quickly take your outfit from chic to scruffy. To protect against this, I recommend carrying a highly effective stain pen (I like to use Tide to Go).

Black & White

Berkeley says wearing black and white together can look very chic, but advises wearing the former on top and latter on the bottom, lest it veers towards looking like a waiter's uniform. I love the idea of wearing black and white stripes, perhaps on a long-sleeve T-shirt or knit, to create contrasts. You could also layer up: a T-shirt or vest under a shirt, or a roll neck under a midi dress. Try accessorising with metallics: a silver or gold shoe or bag looks great with both colors. There are infinite combinations to play with here, all of which are black and white—but never boring.

3

wear the
TROUSERS

"Nothing is more beautiful than freedom of the body."

Coco Chanel

By now, we are getting a picture of Chanel as somewhat renegade: a designer who stuck to her style principles regardless of what anyone else thought or was doing at the time. She was someone who placed little value on trends (unless they were dictated by her, of course) and never shied away from voicing her disapproval of garments everyone else thought terribly fashionable. She never feared being different and never questioned her own ideology—not when it came to women's wardrobes, anyway.

There is no item of clothing that better exemplifies this rebel attitude than trousers. No, really. Jeans, cargo pants, culottes, and chinos might not seem like a daring choice in a contemporary wardrobe, but they are a perfect example of something Chanel thought was essential garb at a time when no one else did. She adopted trousers when they were really only worn by men and championed them throughout her career, fashionable or not.

This loyalty began as soon as she was out of her dreary convent and school uniform. Chanel had graduated from her orphanage at eighteen years old to a Catholic boarding school and then to life as a shop assistant in Moulins. Thus began Chanel's adult life: she lived above said shop on the Rue de l'Horloge with her paternal aunt Adrienne who was just one year older than her (her absent father was one of nineteen children). Even after he abandoned her, Chanel was occasionally in touch with her grandparents, and she and Adrienne had grown close.

It wasn't long before Chanel and Adrienne were introduced to the nightlife scene by some of the town's posted officers (Moulins was a military-heavy town) and began singing regularly at popular spots. In fact, this hobby is rumored to be the provenance of Chanel's legendary nickname, for one of her preferred songs was about a girl who had lost her dog, "Qui Qu'a Vu Coco?" Mind you, this is something the designer has always denied.

We've not yet gotten to the trousers. But this preamble is important, because it was during this period that Chanel met an officer who would influence the course of her life and style. Enter Étienne Balsan, that young textile heir we heard about in chapter one, who swept Coco off her feet and invited her to come and live with him. It was at his impressive home, a former abbey named Royallieu, that Chanel first embraced her androgyny—and realized the power of its contrast.

She was just one of the women milling around Balsan's estate. There were courtesans, too. But where they wore restrictive corsets, cumbersome crinoline, heavy furs, and scratchy lace, Chanel preferred her own tomboy look: riding

Moulins, France, around 1900

breeches and jackets, ties and Peter Pan-collared white shirts. This in part was practical: they better suited her equestrian hobbies in Balsan's stables. But more so, they spoke to her desire to move freely. She was not interested in being restricted by her clothes. She saw how easily men moved in the world and just borrowed from them—often literally.

This made her stand out. But that didn't mean her look caught on. I rather imagine Chanel's outfits at the time were eyed dubiously by her contemporaries. In fact, Chanel would not popularize her trousers for the masses until many years later when she was up and running as a couturier. Of course, she did not invent the concept of trousers for women—the item had already earned a place in their wardrobes during the First World War, when they began undertaking men's work. But she did pioneer them as a chic choice.

Chanel with Étienne Balsan (center) at Château de Royallieu

There is one pair in particular that caught the attention of the world. Around 1930 Chanel was pictured standing next to a Speedo-sporting Duke Laurino of Rome on the Venice Lido. In the sand, she wears white, wide-leg flowing pajama trousers with a black sweater, pearls, cuffs on her wrists, a white and black beret, and espadrilles.

The trousers, of course, were of her own design – and soon everyone wanted a pair. Through the subsequent decade the item became a uniform for starlets: Greta Garbo wore Chanel trousers; so did Marlene Dietrich. Chanel herself had a style for every occasion, be they embroidered for evening or made in navy jersey for lounging around her holiday home, Villa La Pausa, at Roquebrune-Cap-Martin.

Chanel continued to include trousers in her collections even when they were no longer considered modish. This was particularly contentious in the Swinging Sixties, when mini-skirts took hold. The young, hip, and wealthy flocked to Yves Saint Laurent for them – but Chanel loathed the miniskirt. It was her view that knees weren't supposed to be shown off. Besides, she had garnered a statesmanlike clientele of politicians' wives and royals who couldn't be seen in anything so daring. As an alternative (or, perhaps, retaliation) Chanel designed knee-length Bermuda shorts.

Her successors have had no such issues with knees. Miniskirts abound in Chanel collections designed by Lagerfeld and Virginie Viard. But trousers have remained a house code. From baggy and bright pink to logo-laden and skin-tight; cropped at the calf or at the knee like those legendary Bermudas, Chanel trousers continue to offer women the freedom of movement they always have. More than that – they lend the wearer an attitude.

Finding the Right Pair

Trousers are, I think, one of the most difficult items of clothing to shop for. Too long or too short; cutting you off in the wrong place or bagging and sagging in others. What looks wonderful on one person can have the opposite effect on another. With the wide variety of shapes, proportions, and fabrications on offer, working out which pair will look best on you requires some thought. Plus, as with any garment, there are so many different styles in stores. Inevitably you are going to own more than one pair—there's the office, weekend, and cocktail hour to consider.

All that said, you will know the right pair when you put them on. Trousers can be transformative—elegant, polished, sexy and cool in one fell swoop. The guide on the next page, compiled by *The Times* contributing Style Editor and Personal Style Consultant Prue White (who has found the perfect trousers for celebrities on glossy magazine fantasy photo shoots and real-world women seeking them out for their wardrobes), is designed to help you find them.

Body Shape

Body shapes—especially fruit comparisons—can feel dated. But we all feel better when we look good, so when naming our body types it is less about comparing and more about understanding our individual bodies. A lot of it is mathematical—and about maintaining balance and proportions of the silhouette. The "rule of three" is enormously helpful in doing this. You should consider the shoulders, waist, and hips and how they relate to each other, both in terms of ratio and the distance between them.

Triangle

The beauty of a triangle body is a narrow waist relative to wider hips. Always go for a high-rise trouser that will show it off, and be sure to tuck your top in, so that the dramatic ratio is on show. Trousers that hug the bottom gently, without being tight, and then fall into a straight or flared leg will be pleasing to the eye. Additionally, teaming a lighter-colored top with a darker pair of trousers will help to balance a "bottom"-heavy silhouette.

Circle

As with all elements of style, you want to avoid drawing horizontal lines across your widest points. This isn't limited to stripes but extends also to hemlines and waistbands. For jeans, opt for a mid-rise that won't cut across your tummy. In trousers, seek out styles made in a more fluid fabric that falls straight down from the hips (Lyocell fabric is great for this)—in other words, a straight or wide-leg silhouette. Avoid balloon or carrot-leg trousers that will mirror the roundness through your middle, thereby accentuating it.

Rectangle

Rectangular bodies are quite straight up and down, with no defined waist. You want a trouser that contrasts with this. Look for styles in fluid fabrics, perhaps with a pleat front, that will soften the lines of the body. If you do go for pleat-front trousers, consider going up a size so that the pleats sit flat rather than pulling across the hips, though. Boyfriend jeans that are mid-rise and a little loose are also great for softening the straight lines of the rectangular body.

Hourglass

The hourglass body is already well proportioned, with the bust and hips balanced, so you want trousers that maintain that. High-rise bootleg or flared trousers are ideal. The high waist will make the most of your narrowest point, while the wider hemline on a flare will keep the hips balanced.

Inverted Triangle

We refer to bodies with broader shoulders and narrow hips as "inverted triangles." Knowing that we want to maintain balance, this means building out the bottom half to balance out the broadness of the shoulders. Wide-leg or balloon trousers that are high-waisted will be great at breaking up the slope of the inverted triangle and playing to the "rule of threes." You can also consider trousers in a print or bright color.

ADVICE FOR PETITES

Cropped trousers are the most effective trompe l'oeil when it comes to adding height. Specifically, a high-waisted cigarette trouser that flashes a bit of ankle is ideal. While most trousers are easily altered to fit petite people, avoid flared or bootleg styles as the point at which the trouser starts to flare will fall too low on your leg. Pleat fronts that create vertical lines on the leg will add length, while cuffed trousers that draw a horizontal line on the leg will truncate the legs. Furthermore, anything with too much volume will only shorten the body by creating width rather than height.

Short Body
/ Long Legs

In order to balance a short body with long legs, opt for mid-rise trousers, to steal some length from your legs and donate it to your torso. Longer tops that reach down to the hips will help balance the overall silhouette. Also ensure you've invested in good bras that lift the bust. This will add a little length to your torso and create space around the waist.

Long Body
/ Short Legs

It's often the case that where we are longest we are also our leanest. So if you have a long body and short legs, it's quite likely that you have a slim torso. Make the most of this with a high-rise trouser. Not only will this accentuate your waist, it will also create the illusion of longer legs and more balance overall. It will only have an impact if you're wearing a shorter top or have tucked it in, though. If you're not enamored with the idea of tucking something in all the way, opt for a French tuck. Pocket placement is also important: ensure the back pockets sit fairly high on the bottom. Finally, matching shoe color to your trouser can help to add inches to leg length.

Above all, remember that
Chanel designed trousers
to liberate her customers.
Find a pair you can move in,
that will work when styled
with a number of tops in
your wardrobe, and are
comfortable. If you can't
breathe or enjoy a meal in
them, you've missed the point.

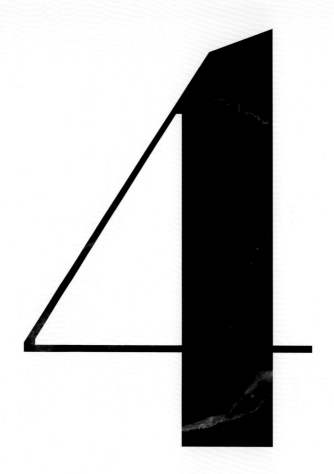

FAKE IT

"A woman needs ropes and ropes of pearls."

Coco Chanel

C hanel had a rather well-known diktat in regard to putting together an outfit. You have probably heard it — it's the sort of quote you see printed out and sold in frames intended for bedroom and dressing-room walls. It instructs that, before leaving the house, one should appraise an outfit in the mirror and remove one accessory. When you consider her approach to jewelry, one might understand why she held such a view.

Chanel did not do dainty gems. She was not one for delicate chains; tiny, rare stones or subtle studs. No, when it came to jewelry, she was all costume: the bigger and bolder the better. It would have been unlikely to have seen her out without her signature wrist cuffs, strings of pearls, or statement brooches and earrings. I am hesitant to use the term *robust*, for the pieces were undoubtedly beautiful, but that's how many of her creations appeared. Some, with their grand-scale designs, metal plating and boiled-sweet gems, looked like armor. They were downright chunky, unapologetically for ornament.

They were also unapologetically fake. That's right: Chanel mainly worked with faux gems, taking the view that to wear precious stones in abundance was a distasteful, flashy display of wealth. That didn't mean that her costume jewelry came cheap (and nor does it to this day). Rather, Chanel elevated it to an art form: her fakes were as desirable as the genuine article—not a faux pas for wannabes. What is compelling is that through this democratization, Chanel reclaimed jewelry for women. No longer was a necklace, brooch, or ring a status symbol that reflected the wealth of the man who purchased it for his wife, mistress, or lover. It was something those wealthy women could buy for themselves to complete a full Chanel look—and wear out and about every day.

At odds with this (for Chanel was never one to shy away from contradiction) was the fact that she did wear real gemstones too—and they were more often than not gifts from her lovers. One man in particular influenced her jewelry design: a Russian emigrant, Grand Duke Dmitri Pavlovich, whom she had known through the 1910s. It is rumored that Chanel turned to Pavlovich for companionship following the death of Boy Capel. It is also rumoured that he fled the Russian revolution with a string of pearls that he subsequently gifted to Coco, and that she then mimicked them so famously for her customers.

There is no Chanel without pearls. They are synonymous with the house and, around Coco's neck, were a signature trademark. In fact, I'd wager that there is no item of clothing that has escaped pearl embellishment at some point in the

brand's history. Young women today might associate traditional strings of pearls with their grandmothers, but Chanel
held the view that they suited everyone. She loved hers so
much that she regularly wore them to the beach, a mark of
how casually she felt jewelry should be treated—and all the
better to flatter one's suntan.

Only on one occasion did Chanel work with real
diamonds, and, true to form, at a moment the world least
expected: November 1932, slap bang in the middle of the
financial crash. Bijoux de Diamants, her only collection of
what fashion refers to as "high jewelry" (that's gem couture,
essentially—items so expensive they don't even have a price
tag), was put on show in Chanel's private rooms at Rue du
Faubourg Saint-Honoré. Thousands of diamonds with an
estimated worth of 93 million francs were shaped into ribbon
bows, feathers, stars, and comets that could be worn inter-
changeably as brooches, hair ornaments, tiaras, and necklaces. As to why a moment of financial austerity prompted
such a luxury-laden statement, Chanel stated that the times
called for authenticity and things of real value. What could be
a more appropriate answer to that than a diamond?

Duke Fulco di Verdura

Later, in the 1930s, another great collaborator on Chanel's jewelry was Duke Fulco di Verdura, a fabulously wealthy Sicilian playboy. The nature of their friendship is largely undocumented (alas, we can but speculate—what we do know is that Verdura had been an aspiring painter and was already working with Chanel on textiles) but the result was lasting jewelry designs. The most famous of these was a baked enamel cuff embellished with colorful gems in the shape of the eight-point Maltese Cross. Nearly as soon as the *bijoux* came into being, two were attached to the wrists of the legendary French–American fashion editor Diana Vreeland—and became the most sought-after jewelry items of the moment. The cross remains symbolic within the house today, most recently knitted as a pattern onto a sweater in the Autumn/Winter 2020 collection.

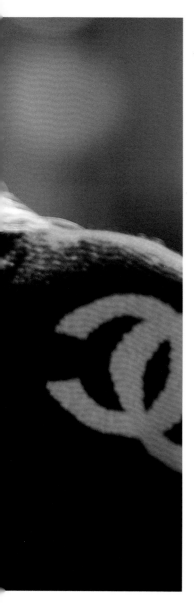

How to Wear Your Jewelry

It is not hard to adopt Chanel's approach to jewelry and, despite what you might think, you don't need to spend a great deal of money in the process. You don't need to buy designer jewelry, nor have the affections of a duke to take advantage of. As with all of Chanel's style principles, it is less about the jewelry itself than how you wear it.

Lesson

1

MIXING YOUR JEWELRY

Lesson one is in becoming a master of mixing high and low. My bet would be that you have at least one very special piece of jewelry. Perhaps it was inherited, given to you by a loved one to mark an occasion, or just gifted to yourself (that, Chanel would absolutely endorse). The quickest and easiest way to appropriate the designer's attitude to bijouterie? Get that item out and start wearing it. Chanel did not approve of keeping precious gems hidden away for special occasions: she wore her real diamonds and pearls with her costume jewelry every day unabashedly, as we have learned. To follow her lead, start mixing in your most valued trinkets with those that you put on as decoration every day.

Lesson

2

MAKE A STATEMENT

Next, learn how to use your jewelry to make a statement. This could be (a) by the design of the jewelry itself or (b) your styling of it. In the first instance, look for pieces that are chunky, colorful, or eye-catching—perhaps those that mix materials unexpectedly or have gobstopper gems (real or not). If you prefer daintier or more delicate pieces, consider route b: piling them on. The following contemporary jewelry styling trends lend themselves to this—Chanel would have more than approved of them.

NECK MESS
wearing several necklaces at once, often on different-length chains and of varying chunkiness, with and without pendants

EAR CURATING
wearing multiple different earrings across several piercings on both ears; ear cuffs are great if you don't have your ears pierced

RING STACKING
wearing several rings stacked together on one finger; you could also wear several rings across both hands

BRACELET LAYERING
stacking cuffs with bracelets and your watch—more is more, all the way up to the elbow if you so desire

Lesson

3

EMBRACE PEARLS

This does not have to be in the traditional sense, though those strings have proven themselves to be timeless. The issue is that they can—in my opinion—be a touch ageing. They bring to mind twinset cardigans, prim WASPs, and Sloanes. But that does not take away from the fact that they suit every skin tone. My suggestion? Look at semi-fine jewelry or high-street fashion brands that have incorporated pearls into modern pieces. Alternatively, seek out baroque and biwa pearls: the classic iteration's cooler, wonky cousins.

Costume Jewelry

You could, if you wanted, seek out original Chanel costume jewelry. Susan Caplan Vintage would be a fine place to start. She is a purveyor of luxury vintage jewelry (her collections are stocked at Selfridges and Harvey Nichols) and an expert in all things Chanel costume. According to her, Chanel pieces are always highly sought after. They are extremely durable, having been dipped in gold several times over during the design process, so they tend to last. The most iconic are those stamped with Chanel's interlocking C logo, and every piece can be styled in multiple different ways: lariat necklaces can be worn down the back, brooches can be used as hair accessories, and necklaces can be layered as bracelets. This, I think, is the most Chanel-esque tip of all: It would truly be in her style to take something and wear it in a totally unexpected fashion.

A NOTE ON METALS

Gold is more dominant in Chanel collections, Caplan says, but it doesn't suit everyone. The rule of thumb is that it works on warmer skin tones, while silver suits those that are cool. Which you might prefer is also a matter of taste: some people find gold tacky and vice versa. The pendulum of which is considered trendy at any one moment in time is constantly swinging. Here, I think we take Chanel's main style principle and apply it yet again: forget what everyone else thinks. Wear what *you* like.

SUIT UP

"Simplicity is
the keynote of all
true elegance."

Coco Chanel

Jackie Kennedy Onassis wore one. So did Princess Diana. Brigitte Bardot, Katharine Hepburn and — during one episode of the cartoon television series in which she exists — even Marge Simpson all had their turn in one. Supermodels and starlets. Politicians and royalty. Wealthy socialites and Wall Street working girls. They all have one thing in common and it, or versions of it, has hung in their wardrobes. What else could it be, but a Chanel suit?

Don't confuse it with the sort you see in most offices. It doesn't have dark pinstripes and is not designed to be worn with a tie. No, Chanel's suits come in a bouclé or tweed, nearly always with grosgrain ribbon trims, and would be remiss without the double-C logo-embossed brass buttons attached. The skirt is usually mid-length and the jacket is cropped. It has a clean silhouette and *always* pockets (reportedly designed to carry Mademoiselle's cigarettes). It's what Coco Chanel is wearing in the first images that appear of her in a Google Images search and what has come to symbolize the epitome of chic the world over. There is no item more iconic, more timeless, or more imitated. It has been turning heads for nearly a century.

Coco Chanel debuted her first tweed suit to the world in the early 1920s. The outfit, a simple collarless jacket with braid trim and a straight-cut knee-length skirt, might sound a bit drab, but—as with all of Chanel's designs—it was downright mutinous to the trends of the day, offering an up-and-down silhouette at a time when the waist was king. Really, only men wore suits—and Chanel's version was borrowed from one man in particular: the Duke of Westminster (or Bendor to his friends).

She was a year into her decade-long love affair with Bendor when she conceived her first suit design. It was a period of Chanel's life in which she spent a great deal of time in the UK. Bendor's two main residences were in Chester (Eaton Hall) and Scotland (Lochmore). At both, Chanel became part of the furniture—and lady of the manor. She embraced country pursuits like fishing and shooting, as well as hosting fabulous parties for the likes of Winston Churchill and putting her stamp on the interiors. She also embraced the duke's wardrobe—all masculine sportswear and tweed. Why, to her mind, should she dress any differently from the men around her?

Chanel began sourcing tweeds from a Scottish mill, where she would bring pink and purple heather as color references, elevating the fabric to unprecedented levels of glamour. She took inspiration from the duke's staff, who wore striped waistcoats. And she began designing suits for

Hugh Grosvenor &

Chanel met the Duke of Westminster, aka Hugh
Grosvenor or Bendor, at a dinner in Monte Carlo
in late 1923. He was married to his second wife
at the time, a fact that didn't stop him wooing
Chanel into an affair—one that lasted ten years
and into his third marriage. Its downfall? The
duke proposed. Chanel said she didn't want to
become yet another Duchess of Westminster.

her customers. The idea for Chanel was that women too should enjoy the freedom of movement and comfort that these garments afforded them without sacrificing elegance. Her first suits were untailored, so there was no constricting waist or whip-tight skirt one couldn't sit down in. The pockets were fit for purpose, so that women would not have to carry a bag. Like so many of her creations, her suit was an act of feminism: one that would be developed to become one of the most celebrated sartorial silhouettes in the world.

That celebration would not hit its true peak until some years later; not in Paris, Scotland, or England, but in America. To understand why, we need to fast-forward to 1954. Chanel had, at seventy-one years old, reopened her couture house. The reasons for it closing in the first place are twofold: first and foremost, the Second World War had broken out—it was "no time for fashion" as Chanel herself stated. But war had not stopped Chanel before. You might remember that during the First World War her business had flourished. The difference this time was that it had coincided with significant damage to her reputation.

This was a complicated period of the designer's history. It's no secret that she had a relationship with a German diplomat during wartime. Hans Gunther von Dincklage, a handsome blond man thirteen years her junior who had worked as a cultural attaché for the German Embassy in Paris and later as a supposed journalist, was known as something of a playboy in Parisian society. He was also a German spy. Chanel's attachment to him raised questions; some believe that, through him, she too was offering her services to Hitler. At the very least, it represented an unforgivable lack of loyalty to France.

One might take the view that she was just trying to survive in occupied Paris. Perhaps, knowing what we do about her approach to life, she thought she was above the

Coco modelling a Chanel suit, 1929

rules of what was considered right at the time, or chose to ignore who and what von Dincklage was, for her own benefit. The truth is that we will never know. She was never officially charged with collaborating. In any case, the damage to her reputation that her choice of lover brought about was enough to force Chanel to close the doors to her shop at 31 Rue Cambon—temporarily. She all but went into hiding in Switzerland, kept afloat by sales of her perfume.

And so we return to 1954, February 5 to be exact, and her reopened salon, where Chanel was presenting her "comeback" collection to the press. The reception was fairly disastrous; all but one, an editor at American *Vogue*, Rosamond Bernier, gave damning reports of what they claimed was a dated and dull collection. They said they had seen it all before—which they had, in a sense. The silhouette Chanel pushed remained the same throughout her career, but now its up-and-down shape pushed back against the hourglass New Look that Christian Dior was enjoying such great success with at the time.

Still, as a designer, Chanel stuck to her guns. Just as well: that one editor, who believed in Chanel's resolute vision that clothes should be easy, was all it took to resuscitate the House of Chanel. She gave Chanel's suits a spread in American *Vogue* and simultaneously to American women, who loved them. It wasn't long before the rest of the world came around again too. By the mid-1960s, seven out of ten suits sold in Paris were Chanel copies.

There was one American woman in particular who loved a Chanel suit. Her name was Jacqueline Bouvier Kennedy (aka Jackie), the wife—and later widow—of President John F. Kennedy. This is ironic given that the first lady wasn't strictly supposed to wear French designers. In fact, when her husband was sworn in, she in turn swore to support and wear American brands. But who can blame her for asking why she shouldn't get to wear Chanel like all the other It-girls of the day? A solution came in the form of Chanel's line-for-line program: the first lady's Chanel suits were designed and cut in Paris, but sent to be sewn together in New York City.

As you do, you might think. But this was a time when such an idea was perfectly acceptable. Until 1978 all Chanel pieces were strictly *haute couture* anyway. The suits took just shy of two hundred hours of manual labor to create. And so it came to be that Jackie Kennedy was wearing one in bubblegum pink with navy trim in Dallas the day her husband was assassinated on November 22, 1963. The image of Jackie Kennedy's Chanel suit splattered with his blood is perhaps the most famous image of the item—if also the most harrowing. That very suit, still stained, remains stored in the National Archives to this day.

How to Wear the Suit

Versions of Chanel's skirt suit abound on the high street every year—but when was the last time you wore one? My guess would be: not lately. Perhaps not ever. Maybe you've bought the little tweed skirt or jacket, but not both. The look might feel too prim or preppy for the weekend yet not quite formal enough for an office. In a world that is increasingly casual—and even Chanel sells jeans—where does a suit fit?

In the case of a Chanel suit, where it always has: as what the personal stylist Annabel Hodin says is "a simple shape with endless versatility." Chanel's suits were designed to give their wearers confidence and to feel comfortable. The point, then, is to find the suit that is the right shape for you. Hodin, who dresses women of all sizes for a living, has these tips:

Avoid skirts that are too long, wide, or tight (like a pencil skirt). A-line and pleat skirts suit most people.

If you are shorter, adapt your skirt length to your height. Skirts below the knee are elongating—mid-calf is particularly flattering.

No matter what size or shape you are, you must have a waist. Make sure your jacket falls there or belt it.

Any shape, especially the hourglass, can wear a fuller skirt with a nipped-in waist, but a larger bust requires a fitted top and a nipped-in waist.

Once you have found your suit, there are endless styling possibilities. The key is wearing it with items that feel up-to-date—perhaps even unexpected. I, for one, like miniskirts—they feel younger and fresh. I also like a boxy cropped jacket. These are the outfits I would wear them with.

Outfit Ideas

Don't feel you have to wear a skirt to get the suited Chanel look. It would be easy enough to swap the miniskirts below for shorts, or the midi skirt for Bermudas or trousers. Whatever you choose, it is the boucle tweed and gold buttons you need to look out for—and there is no end of that combination on the high street.

Jacket	Jacket	Jacket	Jacket
+	+	+	+
shirt	chunky roll-neck knit	white long-sleeve T-shirt	boyfriend shirt (untucked)
+			
sweater vest	+	+	+
+			

MINISKIRT

+	+	+	+
knee-high boot	ankle boot	trainer	chunky loafer

Jacket   **Jacket**   **Jacket, buttoned**

+   +   +

silk shirt   **fine-knit crew-neck**   **silk cami**
sweater tucked in
at the front   +

+   **silk neck scarf**

+   +

KNEE-LENGTH
OR MID-LENGTH SKIRT

+   +   +

slingback block   **loafer**   **slingback block**
or **kitten heel**   or **kitten heel**
or **cocktail flat**   or **cocktail flat**

Finishing Touches

On the question of tights, my advice is to go bare legged where you can. It looks more modern and prevents any chance of your suit looking frumpy. Where that's not possible (or it's just really cold), go for a sheer, low-denier pair with longer skirts; opaque styles look good with minis.

If you can't make the full matching-set look work for you, stick to the tweed jacket. Most Chanel customers that I have spotted in the wild do just that. They are easier to pull off as a single item and look just as good over an office dress as with jeans. Look for boxy shapes, slightly cropped, with front pockets and gold buttons.

Finally, go bold with your jewelry: chunky gold, non-classic pearls, and colourful gems will stop your suit looking too corporate.

Pretty pastels might spring to mind when we think of boucle tweed. But you can still wear the fabric with a bit of edge. Look for styles in navy, black, or white if you're concerned about looking too girly, or jackets with sharp shoulders. What's on trend doesn't apply here: Chanel made tweed tailoring a classic. Find what works for you.

ditch the
STILETTOS

"Shoes . . .
are the last touch
of elegance."

Coco Chanel

C omfort is not stereotypically a sexy word in high fashion — and certainly not when it comes to shoes. This is an industry that invented and enforced the ball-aching stiletto after all; one in which it is not unheard of for glossy magazine editors to actively discourage their editorial staff from wearing flats. In fashion, pain is strangely glamorized: considered a small price to pay for achieving a desired look. Enduring it is what separates the religious fashionista from the rest of us (the former being willing to wear — and bear — anything that their favorite designer has dictated to be on trend). No surprise that Christian Louboutin was able to concede that he does not design his infamous red-soled shoes to be comfortable yet still sells them by the truckload. In recent years, there has been an enormous shift in what the *haute-couture* crowd wear on their feet. Flat sneakers, loafers, ballet flats, and boots are just as, if not more, popular than towering spikes on the front row. If there are heels, they are likely to be walkable: a kitten, blocky, or platform style. But season to season, one shoe remains a must-have with this crowd. It is made by Chanel.

Chanel's bestselling shoe styles don't come with skyscraper heels and never have. In fact, when Mademoiselle introduced her first footwear in 1957 it was in response to her clientele's complaints about the spiked stilettos being popularized by Roger Vivier over at Dior. Unlike those, her now iconic two-tone slingbacks (inspired by the Duke of Westminster's canvas and leather golf shoes), with their blocky low heels, round toes, and delicate straps, were designed entirely with the practicalities of the lives of the women wearing them in mind. As such, they were revolutionary.

Take the heel—its height was chosen to be comfortable enough to walk in but high enough to give the wearer a flattering swing in their step. Beige leather was used to elongate the leg; the contrasting black toe intended to shorten the foot and disguise any scuffs. The elastic strap, an additional touch for comfort, was the work of the man Chanel created the pump with: shoemaker Raymond Massaro. He worked on Chanel shoes until he died in 2019.

Several variations of that legendary pump have followed under Chanel's predecessors, all in the same spirit. Karl Lagerfeld took the iconic two-tone style and applied it to hysteria-inspiring espadrilles, boots, ballet flats, and Mary Janes. He put snow and hiking boots on his catwalks; sneakers, loafers, and chunky-soled, double-strap "dad" sandals too. At Chanel's Autumn/Winter 2022 show, creative director Virginie Viard dressed the models in Balmoral-worthy rubber wellingtons and waders. Who says high fashion cannot be practical? This is not to say that high heels have never graced a Chanel collection. They are simply not standout. The most popular Chanel shoes are also the most functional: consumers desire them not just for their beauty but the way they can imagine wearing them in real life. Mademoiselle famously once said that she could go anywhere with four pairs of shoes—but to my mind, there are nine key Chanel styles to know. You can wear these anywhere, dress them high and low. If you could have one of every pair, you'd have the perfect "cap-shoe" wardrobe.

The Slingback

The original Chanel shoe, the slingback pump comes in several varieties each season, always with an upper in one color or material and a cap toe in another (in the instances both are the same color, the upper is most often leather and the toe a matte grosgrain). The classics come in beige and black—often imitated, never bettered. They always come with a block 65mm heel embossed with a small, discreet double-C logo in gold.

The Mary Jane

Either flat or with a low, blocky heel, Mary Janes have a round or pointed toe and always a strap across the foot (yes, they are a bit like the shoes you probably wore to school). They were a favourite style of Coco Chanel's, who was famously pictured wearing them on the Duke of Westminster's yacht, the *Flying Cloud*. They appeared on runways under Lagerfeld as early as 1989 and in several of his and Virginie Viard's collections since. Those with decorative straps – be they dotted with pearls or bejewelled – are great for parties.

The Ballet Flat

No doubt you've seen Chanel ballet flats in the flesh (or on your social-media feed). They are one of the brand's most popular styles, enjoying their own entire section on its website. Conceived by Lagerfeld just one year into his tenure at the house, Chanel's two-tone ballet flat was a move on from its slingbacks, debuted in his Spring/Summer 1984 collection. It is now a house signature and has been made in every fabric from velvet to tweed.

The Ankle Boot

An ankle boot is very Chanel. Though she never included them in her own collections, Mademoiselle was a huge fan of the style, which she claimed hid her prone-to-swelling ankles. Lagerfeld took the baton, giving them a particularly fabulous moment in the early nineties by shooting them on a string of quilted-leather-clad supermodels astride motor-cycles for the Autumn/Winter 1991 campaign. In the real world, ankle boots are some of the most versatile shoes on the market; they work year-round and look great with almost any outfit or occasion.

The Loafer

Loafers are a later but not less significant addition to Chanel's footwear roster. The first most desired pair, a simple mono-chrome iteration, was introduced as part of the brand's Cruise 2016/2017 collection (famously presented to hundreds of VIPs in Havana, Cuba). Later, chunky-soled black leather styles with gold chain detailing became a must-have; then iterations with a quilted lapel on the front. No matter the design, the Chanel loafer always means business, usually clunky, sometimes platform soled, and always with state-ment hardware.

The Chunky Sandal

They were the sandals that launched a thousand dupes—and forget comfortable, they looked downright orthopaedic. Chanel's "dad" sandals (chunky, Velcro, three-strap crea-tions more closely resembling hiking shoes than footwear costing four figures) were conceived by the brand in 2019 and became single-handedly responsible for making chunky sandals cool. The originals still sell for more than their retail price on second-hand sites; new pairs have waitlists longer than the Nile.

The High Boot

Riding boots, wellington boots, snow boots, and the thigh-length black leather boots Anne Hathaway's character wears after her glamorous makeover in *The Devil Wears Prada*. High boots— that's those long enough to hit just below the knee and above—became part of the Chanel tradition under—you guessed it—Lagerfeld. There seemed no limit to the number of spins he could put on the item, from yeti-esque shearling lined to clear rain boots. But the most epic, I think, came as part of the Autumn/Winter 2017/2018 collection: silver glitter-coated knee-high boots with black cap toes and block heels. Look-at-me, yes—but still made for walking in.

The Espadrille

Mademoiselle wore her espadrilles to the Riviera and Venice Lido with pearls; decades later, Lagerfeld turned them into a viral hit. The two-tone, logo-embroidered, woven raffia-soled shoes débuted on his Spring/Summer 2013 Chanel catwalk to rapture, taking them to far more places than just the beach. Probably just as well, given they only come in leather and tweed these days.

The Sneaker

It seems only right that a brand which prides itself on comfortable footwear should eventually design a sneaker. Actually, it is thought that Chanel was developing one just before she died – a casual jersey shoe to wear on the Riviera. Those available at Chanel today are fit for metropolitan city living. Pioneered by the brand's current creative director, Virginie Viard, they come chunky with quilted soles and even elastic laces.

What all of these shoes have in common is that they are chic but walkable. You wouldn't think twice about slipping them on to get from A to B on foot. Really, the best shoes don't just look good because they have exquisite designs. They do so because the person in them isn't squealing in pain with every step.

seek chic

RIVIERA STYLE

"Fashion is not something that exists in dresses only. Fashion is in the sky, in the street, fashion has to do with ideas, the way we live, what is happening."

Coco Chanel

Psst! Guess what? You probably already own one of the chicest items Chanel put on the fashion map. In fact, were you to conduct an audit of your drawers, I bet you would find more than one. It's long-sleeved, made of cotton jersey, and traditionally comes in navy and white. You can usually spot them at pick-up time at the school gate; ditto at Fashion Week, on the front row. The Princess of Wales has several in her wardrobe, so does Alexa Chung. It is as popular in Cornwall as it is in Paris; is stripy, comfortable, and goes with practically everything. Have you guessed? *Exactement!* It is the humble Breton top.

To clarify: Coco Chanel did not invent it. No—the Breton top (also known as a *marinière*) was already being worn by bohemian types on the Riviera when she adopted it; before that, it was the uniform of French seamen, designed by the brand Saint James since 1858. But she was responsible for making it a high-fashion must-have. More than that, it played a pivotal role in her development as a designer and arbiter of taste. It was the uniform she endorsed when she was off duty, for when Mademoiselle was not in Paris (or, indeed, England, Scotland, or Hollywood), she was sunning her pearls by the sea—on the French Riviera, to be exact.

Cannes. Monaco. Biarritz. Deauville. Chances are you've heard of these coastal hotspots, perhaps even visited them yourself. They are the stages on which the much-desired sartorial genre of French seaside chic has played out, hosting star-studded film festivals, royalty—and the very fabulous. But from as early as 1912 they were, for Chanel, a second home. The designer opened some of her earliest boutiques there, using what was initially an escape from war as an opportunity for expansion. Then, in 1929, she bought her own plot of land on which to build a palatial villa, La Pausa, at Roquebrune-Cap-Martin. It became central to the area's champagne set and who's-who social scene. Of course, they all wore Chanel.

Back to the Bretons. We know that Chanel began her career as a milliner, but it was boyish jersey items that she turned to next. Just before the First World War broke out, she was encouraged by Boy Capel to retreat from Paris to the coast. She found herself in Deauville, Normandy, among droves of wealthy, fashionable women in the same situation—all of whom had wardrobes that needed furnishing.

Never one to miss an opportunity to strike while the iron is hot, in 1913 Chanel set up shop in Deauville, opening her very first ready-to-wear boutique. To fill her proverbial racks there, she set about sourcing jersey (a common material now but at the time used only in the manufacturing of men's

Coco Chanel at home with her dog on the French Riviera

underwear) to create fluid, elegant sportswear inspired by what Capel wore. Suffice to say, it was a hit. Wartime women needed clothes they could do real work in; the wealthy ones wanted unflashy items so as not to appear gauche at a time of national sacrifice. Chanel's pieces—such as the striped *marinière*—offered them that and more: they were practical but elegant; modest items given a stealth luxury spin. You could say they represented a type of fashion manifesto for the rest of her career.

In 1915, a Chanel Haute Couture house in Biarritz followed. She employed three hundred people and an acclaimed all-jersey collection debuted the next year. In 1923 Chanel opened her fourth boutique, in Cannes. Through the 1920s and beyond, Chanel continued to set trends on the Riviera.

Coco Chanel with lover Arthur "Boy" Capel on the beach
in Saint Jean de Luz, 1917

She popularized sunbathing (in pearls), having a tan (not dermatologically advised now), keeping active so as to be lean and athletic. Her social set was actually the first to holiday on the Côte d'Azur during the summer months—prior to that, the area's luxury hotels would close due to the heat. Hard to imagine such an idea now.

Later, inspired perhaps by the uniforms she encountered on staff aboard the Duke of Westminster's yacht, the *Flying Cloud*, she designed floaty trousers, bathing suits, sandals, tennis dresses, and shorts in navy and white. Chanel was democratic, she did not care how humble a clothing item's origins might be, so long as said item was, to her mind, tasteful—and right for that moment in time. Chanel understood which way the wind was blowing, so to speak, in society. She could tell people what they wanted before they knew they wanted it. So it was that she elevated the Breton top from sailor's uniform to a luxury item—ironically one that has been so diluted over the decades that you can pick one up for a snip on the high street.

The Breton stripe has been appropriated time and again in Chanel collections. Viard included striped sweaters in her Spring/Summer 2020 collection. On Lagerfeld's Resort 2019 Chanel runway, models wore navy and white striped trousers with "La Pausa"-emblazoned cream crew-neck knits. But of all the interpretations there is one Chanel Breton top more desired than any other. It was a limited edition as part of the brand's Christmas 2008 capsule collection, and it was gifted to the upper echelons of the fashion industry and friends of the brand. To the untrained eye it looked like any other *marinière*, bar two things: a whacking great double-C logo graffiti-sprayed on the front and a large white Chanel label sewn onto the upper right arm. You cannot buy it now—even on second-hand websites, the item is scarce. You'd have a better chance of finding buried treasure.

How to Wear Stripes

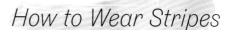

There are no hard and fast rules when it comes to a Breton. It is my firm belief that they look good on everyone and can be appropriated for every setting with any outfit. But not every outfit would be a *Chanel* Breton outfit. And not every Breton is created equal. Breton stripes come on all sorts of garments these days, but Coco Chanel's only came in their purest form: on a long-sleeve, scoop, or crew-neck top in navy and white. Thus, were you to be a purist, you would avoid any iterations with gold buttons, different color stripes or sleeve lengths—and you would follow the styling rules outlined on the following page:

1 Size up

Chanel wore her Breton slightly oversized, all the better to enhance her boyish look.

2 Get your stripes right

Traditional Bretons come strictly with a 2-cm white stripe, followed by a 1-cm blue stripe, and twenty-one stripes in total.

3 Wear by the sea

Chanel and her contemporaries only wore their Breton tops on holiday; the item was considered resort wear.

Now, that is all well and good. But there is so much more you can do with this garment—and it is very much city wear these days. Fashion editors consider Breton stripes a neutral; that means they can be paired with practically anything. A *marinière* is one of the most versatile items one can own and hugely democratic, in the sense that it is fail-safe. Below are just a few combinations that you could style one with: by no means an exhaustive list—but a jumping-off point.

Bottoms

Chanel was famously pictured at La Pausa wearing her Breton with wide-leg, high-waisted trousers and a belt. But you can also wear your Breton with blue or white jeans, shorts, any length skirt, or overalls.

Layering

Bretons look fabulous under blazers and trench coats; ditto under relaxed suiting. You could wear one over a shirt, or under a block-colored sweater with its sleeves rolled up (the striped arms peeping out beneath will add interest, an easy stylist's trick). For an even more nautical look, sling your sweater over your Breton-clad shoulders with the arms of the sweater knotted at the front.

Color Matching

It goes without saying that Breton stripes work well with the colors they come in: navy and white. But don't feel you need to be limited to those. They look fabulous with jewel tones: emerald green, raspberry pink, and ruby red. Metallics work, too, as does—don't think I'm totally mad here—leopard print. You could incorporate these colors via the separates you pair your top with, or the accessories: jewelry, bags, or shoes. For the quickest contrasting pop of color, grab some red lipstick.

I hope this makes clear just how useful a Breton stripe top is. They are the most reached-for thing in my wardrobe; fuss-free and timeless in equal measure. The problem is that they are so handy that they are also highly addictive. It feels impossible to own just one *marinière*; once you start collecting them, it is hard to know when to stop. On this, I can't give any advice. You'll just have to exercise your own restraint.

get a
FLAP BAG

"In order to be irreplaceable, one must always be different."

Coco Chanel

Designer handbags are not any old receptacles. Once they have a luxury logo and monster price tag attached, they gain a kind of magic power for the wearer — and a plethora of symbolic meaning. To your average fashion admirer, they are first and foremost a mere pipedream. You won't get much change out of $9,700 or more for most iterations from Chanel, which rather puts them beyond most budgets. To others, bagging one might be a mark of achievement: something that has been saved for, received as a reward, or in celebration of a milestone. They are obviously a symbol of wealth and status (yet not always an indication of taste). What they are rarely glamorized for is their original function: to carry things.

Not Chanel's iconic bag (well, not in her eyes, at least). Yes, her suits might have come with pockets designed to render the need for a handbag redundant, but she went one step further in February 1955 when she debuted her legendary 2.55 bag (named after the month and year in which it was made). Chanel had been designing matchy-matchy clutches to go with her outfits since the 1920s, but this new bag was a different breed. Once again it ripped up the rule book on what women were toting at the time and was born out of a sheer frustration with it. In true Chanel style, it became the only bag she would ever, in her view—and later those of millions of others—need. The 2.55 was made with what might be inside it in mind.

There are three key design features of the 2.55 that were born purely out of practical needs. The first is the very thing we take for granted on modern bags: the strap. Before Chanel introduced the 2.55, fashionable women carried their possessions in clutches in their hands. The reason Chanel wanted to put paid to that is because, quite fabulously, she kept losing hers. She would put it down and forget about it. The 2.55's leather and metal braided strap not only meant it could be worn over one's shoulder, across the body, or on the hook of the elbow so one could be hands free, but meant the metal didn't clink.

Next, the pockets. The 2.55 came lined with bold red grosgrain or leather and lots of compartments, so that women could find what they were looking for more easily. There were different inner pockets for their keys, cash, cigarettes, or lipstick, plus an extra sleeve on the back. The rectangular shape meant that much could fit in it, and the flap, with its specially designed "Mademoiselle lock," kept items safe but easily accessible.

Aesthetically, the bag held many codes. The now globally recognized quilting, or *matelassé*, on the lambskin leather, silk velvet, and jersey that the bag came in (each intended to suit different times of day) was said to be inspired by that which was worn by the stable boys Chanel learned to ride with on Étienne Balsan's estate. The metal hardware held equestrian memories too, reminiscent of harnesses and bridles. It originally came in the designer's favorite shades: navy, black, beige, and brown. Most significantly, it didn't come with a large, interlocking double-C back then. It was yet another master class in stealth luxury and so successful that it didn't need a logo anyway: the item was instantly recognizable for its look, rather than its label.

When Chanel was urged to design more handbags, she refused. She saw no need for any other style in her life than the 2.55. Karl Lagerfeld didn't quite agree. He has made Chanel bags in the shape of milk cartons, wire grocery baskets, giant Hula-Hoops, and Russian dolls. Virginie Viard's generation of Chanel handbags can't speak much to practicality either. At the brand's Cruise show in Monaco in May 2022, models had tiny bags in the shape of racing-driver helmets, slot machines, and packs of playing cards, roughly large enough to house a packet of Tic Tacs, dangling from their shoulders on gold chains. Forget holdalls—these were hold-nothings.

In February 2005, fifty years after its launch, Lagerfeld reissued the 2.55. You can buy it now in mini and maxi sizes, and the gold chain is no longer braided with leather. With its pockets, quilting, minimal branding, and classic color schemes, it remains an ever-after It-bag to this day—of course, if you can afford it.

The Right Bag

If one is to get the Chanel 2.55 look without investing the money, the handbags in question have to hold five qualities. Undoubtedly, due to Chanel's 2.55 influence, those are very easy to find.

1

No obvious branding
Find a bag that is made of good-quality
leather (or vegan leather if you prefer) with
not-too-flashy hardware and no logos.

2

An adjustable strap
You want to be able to wear your bag
multiple ways—extra marks if the strap
is a gold chain.

3

Pockets
Your bag should be practical, with plenty
of places to put things.

4

Quilting
Self-explanatory—find something
that mimics the 2.55's pillowy
diagonal texture.

5

A flap and lock
The bag should have a flap closure, ideally
with a metal twist lock to close it.

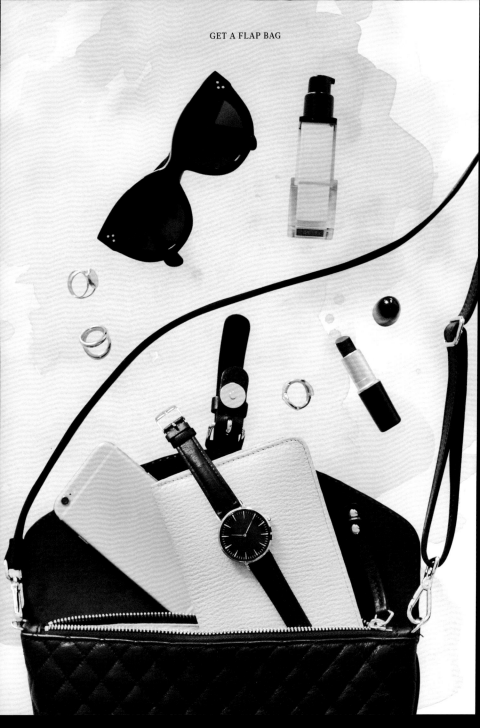

GET A FLAP BAG

Once you have found your bag, you just need to decide how to wear it. To my mind, there are three ways that maintain Chanel's bid for her customers to be hands free.

CROSS BODY

The easiest way to wear your bag is with the strap long, diagonally across your body. This looks great over an outfit when you are out and about or commuting and adds a point of interest, particularly when the bag has a metallic chain—a bit like jewelry.

ON THE SHOULDER

An elegant way to wear your bag is over one shoulder, with the bag long or short. A short chain will allow you to clutch the bag under your armpit, too, for extra security. A longer chain will mean it swings as you walk and is easily accessible.

ELBOW HOOKED

Perhaps the most prim—read, high-maintenance—way to wear your bag is over the hook of your elbow. It doesn't leave you totally hands free, but is a pose the style set makes use of when they are texting (and want to show their designer bag off to anyone watching).

Whichever bag you choose and however you choose to wear it, the key principle of a Chanel bag is that it makes your life easier. If it's not allowing you to move more smoothly in the world, with easy access to your prized possessions, then it isn't right. But keep in mind that it should also glean the odd desiring glance from strangers. It should be beautiful, well-made, and downright happy-making. In short, your bag should be functional, yes—but it should not be an old rucksack.

borrow from
THE BOYS

"*Men always remember a woman who caused them concern and uneasiness.*"

Coco Chanel

Coco Chanel was a woman of striking character with a resolute sense of self. She did not take the world as it was but instead sought out and fashioned ways in which it could be—to her mind—better. She behaved, dressed, and held herself not as she should or was expected to in the eyes of society, but exactly as she pleased.

She was considered, as her business grew, a New Woman: independently wealthy (independent full stop). She took lovers, never married, traveled, and distilled her ideas around the globe, all the while telling the world her own versions of stories about her life because the truth simply did not suit her. She acted, by and large, in her own inter-ests and moved confidently up through the ranks of society without any sense of self-doubt or impostor syndrome (not that she let on about anyway). She was a woman, yes—but she behaved like a man.

We know that Chanel borrowed from the wardrobes of the men in her life. Her two-tone slingbacks were inspired by the Duke of Westminster's golf shoes. Suits and trousers were stuck in men's wardrobes before she glamorized them. Breton tops were for fishermen; quilting for stableboys. Even the designer's use of proper pockets was novel in female clothing at the time.

Jewelry, before she set her mind to it, was something women had bought for them by men. The cardigan is said to have emanated from those worn by English cricket players—Chanel adopted it because she didn't like the way tight-necked sweaters would mess up her hair when being pulled over the head. As for hair, she was one of the first women to wear hers super short and gamine. She cut it herself.

But all of this was not about looking or feeling masculine. Quite the opposite. The garments and accessories Chanel created were undeniably feminine. They may not have given the wearer hourglass silhouettes or buxom cleavage, but they were deeply elegant and pretty. The shape and structure of her clothes derived from those hanging in men's wardrobes, but came adorned with shiny buttons, ribbons, and delicate details; perhaps finished with a camellia flower as a buttonhole on the lapel. What they took from menswear was an attitude: a Chanel item gave women the freedom of movement and functionality that men enjoyed from their clothes and which they had previously been denied.

From the early 1900s Chanel rejected the commonplace idea that the way women dressed should be a representation of their relationship to men. While most twenty-somethings wore ornate gowns and corsets to the races, bought for them by their husbands, fathers, or lovers, Chanel wore jackets

I bet you didn't think cardigans started life in men's wardrobes. Perhaps you even considered them the reserve of grandmothers—particularly when worn with pearls. Think again. You can inject them with a bit of va-va-voom. V-neck styles worn with nothing underneath or oversized takes worn off the shoulder are a favorite modern look. Wear it tucked into the front of your jeans to show off your waist and you're away.

and ties purloined from the men in her life. Keep in mind that this was the period in which she was kept by Étienne Balsan, so her situation was no different from other mistresses. But her wardrobe was. In wearing Balsan's clothes instead of those which he hypothetically could have bought for her, she marked herself out. She was not another woman in whalebone, thickly powdered with rouge. As such, people did not know what to expect of her. She defied the norm and I suspect it gave her control.

So, the concept of borrowing from the boys went beyond clothes for Chanel. That much is obvious. It was about the attitude that the clothes offered — a posture. Or postures. Indeed, if we study images of Chanel, she is rarely captured in a pose that does not ooze confidence. There are several gestures that appear time and again in portraits of the designer, none of which scream of traditional femininity.

Often, she would have her hands shoved deep into her pockets. She would stand with one or both hands on her hips, stood either straight or with a hip cocked ever so slightly to the side. When she sat, she crossed one leg over the other. She maintained a straight posture and held her cigarettes aloft. Sometimes her arms would be crossed, not in a defensive way, but with easy self-conviction.

Chanel campaigns tell a similar story. The Chanel woman in her most concentrated form exudes a knowing confidence. See Kate Moss sat barefoot in a silver dress with her legs tucked beneath her — not in a neat crouch, but manspreading — for Spring/Summer 2004. Or Claudia Schiffer for Spring/Summer 1995, stood with her forefingers tucked into the front pockets of her lilac tweed dress, hip jutted and elbows out. Cara Delevingne leans on the ropes of a boxing ring, arms draped leisurely, for Autumn/Winter 2014. For Spring/Summer 2002, Stella Tennant marches alone, head down, through the streets of Biarritz.

Chanel designed clothes for the woman she wanted to be: someone who knew what she wanted, where she was going, and how to take up space in the room when she arrived. I am conscious that this is all starting to sound a little whimsical. But fashion is a powerful, transformative beast. Chanel knew the power that garments could have. We all do: there is nothing worse than feeling uncomfortable. By taking what were considered masculine garments and reframing them for women, Chanel was able to change the way women held themselves and to usher in the era's New Woman, who had her own bicycle, cigarettes, and job.

So much of Chanel's borrowing from the boys was a search for practicality. I am at risk of repeating myself here, but let me labor the point anyway: women's clothing did not, at this point in time, make any functional sense. When Chanel designed ankle-skimming dresses in 1916, it was the first time women did not have to lift their skirts to climb up a step. Her heels were made for walking in; the pockets on her jackets for filling. These are things that we take as read in the modern woman's wardrobe. It cannot be understated how influential Chanel was in ushering them in, from one gender's cabinet to the other.

Ready to Wear

Borrowing from the boys is not a groundbreaking concept in today's world—and not just because western women have been daring to wear more than skirts and dresses for a good century or so. We live in far less traditionally gendered times than Chanel did. The concept of gender itself is a white-hot cultural topic of the twenty-first century and individuals identify by their own rules, not biology.

That in mind, how we wear clothes—be they labeled menswear or womenswear—is a far more open-ended brief. Hard and fast diktats no longer apply, unless you are in a fusty members' club with a stringent dress code. Designer collections are largely presented as gender-neutral now, with models of all pronouns walking the catwalk. Chanel's website diplomatically refers to its clobber as "ready-to-wear" rather than "womenswear." The fashion industry at large has embraced the zeitgeist for avoiding gender labels, which feels representative of the community it fosters: for all of the rules it sets about what's hot and what's not, it has always been a safe harbor for those who break them.

That said, we can approach the concept with a light touch. There are garments that were originally designed for men that have come to be major players in women's wardrobes. This is a capsule of my top five.

The Blazer

Boxy, cropped, and double-breasted or broad and power-shouldered—you can take your pick when it comes to blazers: they are difficult to get wrong. There is a reason the tailored jacket is part of every fashion editor's uniform; come to a catwalk show and see how many are shrugged over the shoulders of those sitting in the front row if you want proof. My advice is to find one that is structured and boxy with sharp shoulders (note: nothing waisted) in black, navy, or a pinstriped wool blend. Bouclé nods to Chanel's tweed suits; a Prince of Wales or houndstooth check with elbow patches harks back to her country pursuits with the Duke of Westminster. Velvet options are high glamour and lovely in winter time. Style any of these over a coordinating plain T-shirt or shirt, or fully fastened over a silky camisole (or nothing at all) for a racier evening take.

The Loafer

A bit bookish, a bit house slipper, the loafer is one shoe that has yet to fall out of fashion with the style set over the past near-decade. Their favorite pairs come in butter-soft black or cream leather with gold hardware. You can't go far wrong following that, but I think they also look good in a bright color—red or green—or metallic. Chunky-soled iterations are good if you prefer stomp or a bit of height.

Style Tip
add a brooch or buttonhole

Style Tip
wear with bare legs

The Three-piece Suit

Do not be afraid of the three-piece suit—it is not as corporate, buttoned-up, or high maintenance as you think. Worn together, the jacket, trousers, and vest look polished and powerful; separately they are three singular tailored items that will work hard in the rest of your wardrobe. The style set wear their three pieces with sneakers or heels and nothing underneath: less boardroom, more Left Bank. A suit and tie will channel Diane Keaton in *Annie Hall.*

Style Tip
add a silk scarf
or beret

The Boyfriend Shirt

Crisp, polished, a bit sexy—and never the sort that would strain over one's bust—a straight up and down mannishly tailored shirt should be in every woman's wardrobe. The key is to find one that is slightly oversized (never tight) and a bit boxy. Avoid styles with darting, stretch fabric, or rounded hems, and opt for white, pale blue, or striped Oxford styles. Linen or silk are more flattering, fluid options for larger busts. Oversized cuffs look lovely but can be irritatingly floppy. French-tuck your shirt into the front of your bottom half (leaving the rest of the shirt loose), undo a few buttons, and roll up the sleeves to add shape.

Style Tip
wear with strings of pearls or a gold chain

The Jumpsuit

The original jumpsuit came in functional fabric and was designed so that parachuters could leap from planes. Chanel's versions, designed under Karl Lagerfeld and Virginie Viard's tenures, are a touch more glamorous—they have been worn by the likes of J.Lo, Cardi B and Gigi Hadid on catwalks and red carpets. For the rest of us they make great throw-it-on alternatives to dresses in that they create a complete outfit in one fell swoop. Evening options are high-octane; daytime versions make one feel one can conquer anything (except making a quick trip to the restroom). I like denim, velvet, and corduroy iterations most: the fabrics are forgiving.

Style Tip
wear with a chain belt on the waist or hips

The above can all be mixed and matched seamlessly into your wardrobe—you can style them up with basics, layering, jeans, for work, or weekend. How oversized you want to go with them is a personal choice. A little boxiness is elegant, but you may want to avoid the other B: baggy.

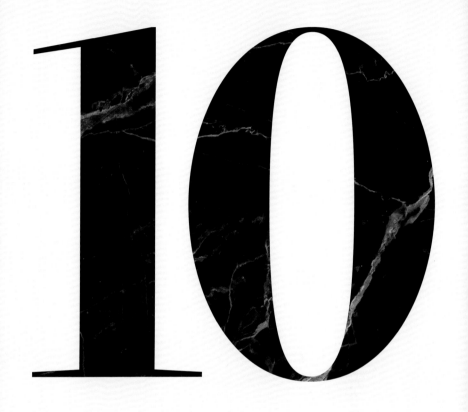

10

spritz, bronze &
ADD RED LIP

"A woman who doesn't wear perfume has no future."

Coco Chanel

A s with all things, Coco Chanel had rules about beauty—and she was steadfast both in keeping to and dictating them. Much like the clothes she designed, the basic principles of her grooming rituals did not change much throughout her life. It is another example of her self-conviction: she had a look (and scent) she liked and stuck to it, not even changing her hairstyle after embracing a bob in 1916.

Besides, she was obviously onto something. When you look at the beauty ideologies and products she espoused, you will probably find you already practice them and/or that they feature on your bathroom shelves. Her approach to beauty was a simple one—that it should be done as an act

of self-care. There was no mood that could not be marginally improved upon by spending ten minutes perking up how one looks, she thought.

Most icons have signature looks. When we think of Anna Wintour, we picture her glossy bob and black sunglasses. Donatella Versace is known for her platinum-blonde hair and nude lipstick. Marilyn Monroe (more on her later) had her beauty spot and golden curls. In addition to Chanel's dark crop, there are three things she was known for. The way she smelled—always of her own perfume, Chanel No. 5. Her bronzed skin—she made having a suntan desirable. Finally, her crimson lips; she was rarely seen without a slick of red lipstick on, the ritual of applying which she compared to putting on armor.

Today, fragrance and beauty is an enormous part of the Chanel organization: if you can't afford to buy the house's clothes and accessories, you can probably treat yourself to a bottle of nail polish. The products it offers continue to celebrate its founder's beauty principles. Below are their stories, with tips on how to bring them into your own routine.

WEAR PERFUME

A bottle of it is sold every thirty seconds and it was famously the only thing Marilyn Monroe wore to bed. Just over a century ago, Chanel No. 5 changed the way the world thought about perfume forever—and it was all down to that knack of its creator for breaking and remaking the status quo.

Chanel loved perfume. She had a hypersensitive sense of smell and strong opinions about who and what was "clean." Couturiers were already creating house fragrances when she, at the age of forty, finally set about formulating and selling her own. But those available on the market were by and large basic flower potions. Chanel didn't want her signature scent to have one note; she wanted it to be complex—to represent the modern woman. As it is, Chanel No. 5 is made up of over eighty natural and synthetic ingredients—which helped it live up to Coco's desire that it be the most expensive perfume in the world.

Chanel did not create the scent. It was a French perfumer by the name of Ernest Beaux who devised its formula. He set himself apart from his contemporaries in the field with his understanding of organic compounds called aldehydes to keep perfume stable (thereby making it last longer once out of the bottle). He created a selection of samples for Chanel to pick from. She chose the golden liquid in vial number five.

That is one theory on how the perfume got its name. Another is that Chanel was superstitious and had been told by a fortune teller that five would be her lucky number; Chanel herself is also a Leo—the fifth Zodiac sign. In any case, the name of the perfume and the elegant Art Deco bottle it came in, itself a contrast to the (literally) overblown romantic vials other perfumes available at the time came in, was an instant hit. It remains universally recognizable globally—Chanel still refers to it as its treasure.

In 1952, Marilyn Monroe—then the most famous woman in the world—was photographed for *Life* magazine spritzing herself with a bottle of Chanel No. 5 after being quoted in the accompanying interview saying it was the only thing she wore to bed. Chanel would go on to release six more scents before her death, including one for men. Today, the house of Chanel offers more than twice as many scent franchises for women alone and a further portfolio for men, so you have a wealth to choose from if you want to find one for yourself.

When you do—or wherever you get your perfume—there is only one rule per Chanel's style principles: wear it.

How to Achieve the Chanel Look

Get a tan (or fake it)

Chanel was one of the first women to popularize having a glowing tan. Before that, glamorous types would never have dreamed of it: pale skin was a symbol of nobility and an easy life spent indoors. Not once Coco Chanel came on the scene. In a testament to the designer's influence at her peak, it only took her being photographed disembarking a cruise in Cannes after catching too much sun in 1923 for her to set a new beauty standard: pale out; glowing in. She maintained that a suntan was an easy way to enhance one's natural beauty. It's why she spent so much time outside when at her holiday home on the Riviera and why she wore white pearls when she did so: they accentuated her bronze.

Dermatologists might disagree with her methods now, but there are plenty of ways to get a glow without frequenting the sunbed. Fake tan is the obvious one: I recommend using a mousse, a mit to apply it, and exfoliating and moisturizing the night before for an even and streak-free application. Tan drops that can be mixed in with moisturizer are a brilliant and quick overnight solution for the face (just don't forget to wash your hands well afterwards).

For less dramatic effects, consider how to get a healthy glow from your makeup bag. The British makeup artist Julia Wren, who works with celebrities, models in fashion campaigns, and one-to-one with real women, says that bronzer is the perfect solution— but don't cover your entire face in it. She suggests sweeping it where the sun naturally tans your skin— a little sweep at the top of your forehead near your hairline, a sweep to the top of your cheeks, and across the bridge of your nose.

She most highly recommends a cream bronzer for its natural look and how well it blends and settles into lines and wrinkles. (My favorite is actually from Chanel's Les Beiges collection, a line designed to give the wearer a bronzed radiance, but any bronzer will do.) Powder bronzers are great for touch-ups— Wren suggests using a fluffy brush and starting with a little product at first and building it to your desired shade. Finally, those with more mature skin should avoid anything with glitter and sparkle—matte is much more flattering.

Add a slick of lipstick

Chanel was a great advocate of makeup. In fact, she was against leaving the house without it—to do so, she thought, was tasteless. This goes some way to explain why the designer nearly always sported a red lip, the power of which she expressed by once saying, "If you're sad, if you are disappointed in love, put on your makeup, give yourself some beauty care, put on lipstick, and attack."

Naturally Chanel thought she could offer something better than what was on the market. In 1924 she introduced an ultra-pigmented, creamy lip color collection for her customers and a bespoke crimson shade for herself: Premier Rouge.

Then, the lipsticks came in mother of pearl tubes; today, they come in unmistakable black and gold logo-stamped casing. They remain some of the most iconic lipsticks of all time.

A red lip can feel intimidating. Not only that, they are high-maintenance: you need to keep an eye on them and they often need to be touched up. That said, they are a powerful thing when done right.

To do that, Julia Wren says that you need to determine your skin undertone (we did this in chapter one). As well as the paper test, her great tip is to consider what type of jewelry most flatters you: if it is gold, you are probably warm; silver

Which Shade of Red to Choose

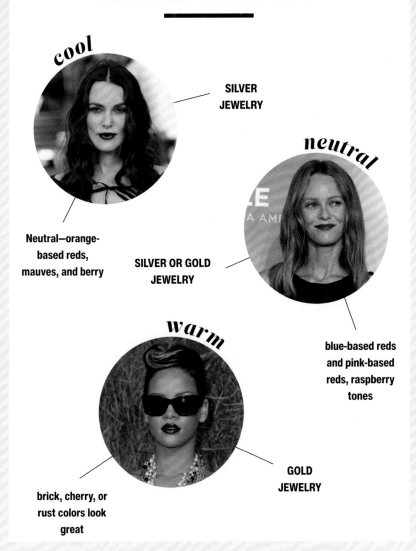

cool

SILVER
JEWELRY

neutral

Neutral—orange-
based reds,
mauves, and berry

SILVER OR GOLD
JEWELRY

blue-based reds
and pink-based
reds, raspberry
tones

warm

GOLD
JEWELRY

brick, cherry, or
rust colors look
great

is cool and if you suit both, you have a neutral skin undertone.

Once you have worked that out, she says, you can use the guide on page 183 to work out which shade of red to choose.

In addition to this, I suggest finding a lip liner in the same shade—you can use it as a matte base layer for your lipstick and to keep the lipstick in place. Blotting is key: I like to use a tissue to do so between layers of lippie to build up the color.

Finally, have fun with it. A red lipstick says party, glamour, confidence, and sexiness. It's everything Coco Chanel wanted her women to be. That might not be something you think you can bottle—but it's a formula the company sells today with every crimson stick.

So now you have a full tool kit for creating your own Chanel look. And it being your own is the very point, by the way. It was not Chanel's style to copy or follow others—we know full well that she put forward an aesthetic that was on her own terms. That in mind, the most Chanel thing you could do is the very same. By that I mean: don't take what you have learned in this book as a set of strict rules. Get inspired by the history and principles. Take note of the practical tips. Then go your own way with them. Offer your own spin. Of all the style principles of Chanel, there is one that binds them all together as the most important: be yourself.

References

Bronwyn Cosgrave, *Vogue on Coco Chanel* (Melbourne, AU: Hardie Grant, 2012).

Lisa Chaney, *Chanel: An Intimate Life* (New York: Penguin, 2012).

Emma Baxter-Wright, *Little Book of Chanel* (London: Welbeck, 2020).

Justine Picardie, *Coco Chanel: The Legend and The Life* (New York: HarperCollins, 2012.)

Miren Arzalluz and Véronique Belloir, *Gabrielle Chanel: Fashion Manifesto*, translated from French by Ruth Sharman (London: Thames & Hudson, 2020).

Quote sources
p.16 Chanel, Coco. *Goodreads.* Available from: https://www .goodreads.com/quotes/515582-a -woman-s-education-consists-of -two-lessons-never-leave-the

p.36 Chanel, Coco. *Goodreads.* Available from: https://www .goodreads.com/quotes/273344 -women-think-of-all-colors -except-the-absence-of-color

p.54 Chanel, Coco. *Quotefancy.* Available from: https://quotefancy .com/quote/788663/Coco-Chanel -Nothing-is-more-beautiful-than -freedom-of-the-body

p.74 Chanel, Coco. *Pearls of Joy.* Available from: https://www .pearlsofjoy.com/blogs/blog/famous -pearl-quotes

p.94 Chanel, Coco. *Goodreads.* Available from: https://www .goodreads.com/quotes/205586 -simplicity-is-the-keynote-of-all -true-elegance

p.112 Chanel, Coco (as cited by Louise Roe). 'British Vogue: Chanel Gets Toned' [website], 2007, https://www .vogue.co.uk/article/chanel-gets -toned (accessed 16 February 2023)

p.126 Chanel, Coco. *Goodreads.* Available from: https://www .goodreads.com/quotes/12859 -fashion-is-not-something-that -exists-in-dresses-only-fashion

p.140 Chanel, Coco quoted in Marcel Haedrich, *Coco Chanel: Her Life, Her Secrets* (New York: Little Brown and Company, 1971).

p.156 Chanel, Coco. *Goodreads.* Available from: https://www .goodreads.com/quotes/491122-men -always-remember-a-woman-who -caused-them-concern-and

p.172 Chanel, Coco. *Goodreads.* Available from: https://www .goodreads.com/quotes/31819 -a-woman-who-doesn-t-wear -perfume-has-no-future

Acknowledgments

Thank you first and foremost to Ru and Lucinda at Ebury for thinking of and working with me on this project, and to Celia for putting us in touch (I will always be pleased I walked into that nail bar and sat next to you!).

Thank you to my brilliant and dear colleagues at *The Times*—to Anna, Harriet, and Nicola for encouraging me, to Hannah and Sidonie for the moral support, and to Jane for your counsel and genius scribbles.

To Awon Golding, Susan Caplan, Anna Berkeley, Camilla Elphick, Annabel Hodin, Prue White, and Julia Wren for your generous time and expertise—I am indebted.

To my parents, Cheryll and Mike, who have always supported and believed in my career.

Finally, to George, who patiently watched me embark on this project in the months and weeks leading up to our wedding, kept me at my desk, boundlessly cheerled from the sidelines, and soothed all anxieties: there will never be enough thank-yous.

About the Author

Hannah Rogers is *The Times*'s assistant fashion editor and stylist and covers whatever is capturing the zeitgeist, specialising in trends, fashion, red carpet, and celebrity. She studied anthropology and sociology at Durham University, followed by an MA in fashion journalism at Central Saint Martins, and has worked in broadsheet journalism for seven years as a writer and stylist. This is her first book.

Photo Credits

Images kindly provided by: Alamy (p.21 The Picture Art Collection and p.129 Granger – Historical Picture Archive); Getty (p.8 Archive Photos; p.12 Sasha; p.14 Daniel Simon; p.18 Heritage Images; p.23 Gerard Julien; p.24 Pascal Le Segretain; p.27 Christian Vierig (top left), Victor Virgile (top right), Christian Vierig (bottom left), Stephane Cardinale - Corbis (bottom right); p.28 Dominique Charriau; p.34 Dominique Charriau; p.39 New York Times Co.; p.43 Victor Virgile; p.46 WWD; p.47 Antonio de Moraes Barros Filho (left), Francois Durrand (right); p.49 Victor Boyko; p.50 Thomas Concordia (left), Bertrand Rindoff Petroff (middle), Pascal Le Segretain (right); p.52 Stephane Cardinale - Corbis; p.57 LL; p.58 Heritage Images; p.61 Claudio Lavenia; p.63 Stephane Cardinale - Corbis; p.64 Stephane Cardinale - Corbis; p.65 Dominique Charriau; p.66 Pascal Le Segretain; p.67 Stephane Cardinale - Corbis; p.69 Christian Vierig; p.70 Joe Maher; p.72 Victor Virgile; p.80 Jeremy Moeller; p.83 Pascal Le Segretain; p.85 Claudio Lavenia; p.86 Christian Vierig; p.87 Bertrand Rindoff Petroff (left), Daniel Simon (right); p.88 Antonio de Moraes Barros Filho; p.92 Dominique Charriau; p.97 Topical Press Agency; p.99 Sasha; p.105 Penske Media; p.110 Pascal Le Segretain; p.121 Edward Berthelot; p.124 Pascal Le Segretain; p.130 Apic; p.132-133 Handout (left), Pascal Le Segretain (middle), Christian Vierig (right); p.137 Victor Virgile; p.138 Jeremy Moeller; p.144-145 Jeremy Moeller; p.146 Edward Berthelot; p.147 Jeremy Moeller; p.150 Streetstyleshooters (left); p.151 Bertrand Rindoff Petroff; p.152 Jeremy Moeller; p.154 Heritage Images; p.162 Edward Berthelot; p.165 Thomas Concordia; p.166 Edward Berthelot; p.167 Jeremy Moeller; p.168 Karwai Tang; p.177 Michael Ochs Archives; p.181 Bertrand Rindoff Petroff; p.183 Julien M. Hekimian (top), Francois Durrand (middle), Pascal Le Segretain (bottom); p.184 Stephane Cardinale - Corbis; p.185 Edward Berthelot (left), Stephane Cardinale - Corbis (right); p.187 Streetstyleshooters); Shutterstock (p.122 Creative Lab); Unsplash (p.44-45 Laura Chouette; p.102 Yves Monrique; p.117 NajlaCam; p.118 Harper Sunday; p.149 Marissa Grootes; p.150 Vladimir Yelizarov (right); pp.170, 174 and 178 Laura Chouette).

SIMON ELEMENT

An Imprint of Simon & Schuster, LLC
1230 Avenue of the Americas
New York, NY 10020

First Simon Element hardcover edition May 2024

SIMON ELEMENT is a trademark of Simon & Schuster, LLC

Simon & Schuster: Celebrating 100 Years of Publishing in 2024

For information about special discounts for bulk purchases, please contact Simon &
Schuster Special Sales at 1-866-506-1949 or business@simonandschuster.com.

The Simon & Schuster Speakers Bureau can bring authors to your live event. For
more information or to book an event, contact the Simon & Schuster Speakers
Bureau at 1-866-248-3049 or visit our website at www.simonspeakers.com.

Manufactured in China

1   3   5   7   9   10   8   6   4   2

Library of Congress Cataloging-in-Publication Data has been applied for.

ISBN 978-1-6680-5449-9
ISBN 978-1-6680-5450-5 (ebook)